How To Sell Products Online Using Social Media

By:
Glenda F. Boone

Terms and Conditions

LEGAL NOTICE

Glenda Boone, the Publisher has strived to be as accurate and complete as possible in the creation of this report, notwithstanding the fact that she does not warrant or represent at any time that the contents within are accurate due to the rapidly changing nature of the Internet.

While all attempts have been made to verify information provided in this publication, the Publisher assumes no responsibility for errors, omissions, or contrary interpretation of the subject matter herein. Any perceived slights of specific persons, peoples, or organizations are unintentional.

In practical advice books, like anything else in life, there are no guarantees of income made. Readers are cautioned to reply on their own judgment about their individual circumstances to act accordingly.

This book is not intended for use as a source of legal, business, accounting or financial advice. All readers are advised to seek services of competent professionals in legal, business, accounting and finance fields.

Glenda Boone

Table of Contents

Foreword	3
Chapter 1: Throw A Game Or Contest	4
Chapter 2: Give Aways	8
Chapter 3: Gain Loyalty By Providing A Stake In The Brand	13
Chapter 4: Build Credibility By Helping Others	17
Chapter 5: Have Some Fun	21
Chapter 6: About The Author	28

Foreword

Social media is in the end about relationships. It should be deemed a two-way street. As a brand, you aren't there to market a product, you're there to communicate and associate. If you attack social media with gross sales as your end destination, your audience will detect it and, most likely, you'll be snubbed.

But, if you provide your audience something valuable, and your message is real, (you aren't manipulating it) consumers are inclined to take heed. Provide users engaging material, helpful info, streamlined client service, or bonuses like discounts and gratis gifts consistently, and you've the makings of a fit long-term relationship with a brand promoter willing to blab your praises to the globe.

After which, as long as you pull your weight by maintaining your message, meaning reliable and meaningful, consumers tend to remain loyal and express that in income generated over time and favorable references expressed amid their peers. That's the true return on social media.

Chapter 1

Throw A Game
Or Contest

Synopsis

Once a voguish women's shoe designer was seeking a way to obtain more business and there was already a favorable buzz surrounding the brand. Their shoes were being featured in fashion magazines. All the same, the designer had only a set reach, so taking advantage of the existing word of mouth by constructing a social media buzz made complete sense.

Create Buzz

The construct was simple. In a "Where Do Your Shoes Go?" contest, users were expected to post pictures of themselves in intriguing locations wearing their designer shoes. Users voted for their preferred pictures and the victors got a year's supply of designer shoes.

The outcome? Gobs of fresh Facebook fans, tens of thousands of intermeshed users, a grounded social-media buzz, and the origination of many useful brand enthusiasts for the industrious designer label. How to do it?

Figure out the particulars of the contest. Find and get a prize that's relevant to the concerns of your brand. Plan for a particular launch date for the contest to become active, and a deadline by which all contestants will have to enter to be eligible to get the prize and any other contest particulars. Get a social media account free using Twitter, Facebook, Myspace, etc. The social site will allow contestants to show their interest in participating.

Announce the competition. Update your social page to advise your visitors that a contest is being held. Include all of the info that the potential contestants will need to know prior to entering the contest. Make your visitors cognizant of the prize, and let them know that they'll need to participate through your social media site. Upon picking out the winner, e-mail him seeking the details of where you are able to send the prize. Pick out runner-ups in the event that you don't hear back from the initial victor of the contest.

Run the contest and pick a winner. Sort through all of the entries you've been sent, and pick out the winner based on the contest rules.

Give out the prize and declare the results. Send off the prize to the winner of the contest, and once he's received the prize, declare the results of the contest on your social media site.

This will see to it that none of your visitors are left ceaselessly wondering whether or not they've been selected as the winner. As well, this will bring people back to check for the next contest and stir interest in your brand and your main web site.

Chapter 2

Give
Aways

Synopsis

If planning and carrying out an online game or competition seems intimidating, you are able to always come back to basics and appeal to a general human reality: individuals love free junk.

Free Stuff

There is another success story with an online photo processing service who wanted to establish a fan base and tug at user engagement via Facebook. What they did was use a monthly e-zine to promote an easy game related to an old classic photo game. In the e-zine, 2 subtly dissimilar pictures were featured, and the 1st groups of users who named and posted the deviations on Facebook got a $25 gift card. The photo processing company got more Facebook fans than ever - or since.

In a like promotion, an alcoholic beverage company discovered a creative way to capitalize on extra canvas carryalls sitting around their office. Instead of stuffing the bags in a storage closet, they utilized the bags as prizes in a competition designed to drive user participation on Facebook.

To acquire a carryall, users were asked to place pictures of themselves drinking the beverage on the brand's Facebook page, a comparatively effortless request looking at the number of drinking photos on

Facebook. Needless to say, the canvas carryalls went like hotcakes, and brand cognizance expanded exponentially. The price? An uncluttered office.

If you're just beginning and not making any income yet on, then you'll have to decide whether or not you prefer to spend money on a giveaway or not.

What should you give away? Gift cards are forever popular. But a different great idea is to target it to your chief audience. Give something away that will associate with your product or service.

Don't prefer to spend your own income on a giveaway? You still have alternatives. Attempt asking business owners that you know if they'd like to sponsor a giveaway. You'll have to pitch your site, so make certain you tell them how many visitors you get or expect. Tell them who you readers are and what kind of products that they'd be interested in. And tell them how you'll market your giveaway. Do make certain to tell them that they'll be responsible for sending the prize to the winner however. It is so much simpler than having them ship it to you and then you sending it to the winner.

Another way to discover sponsors for your giveaways is to ask your contacts on Twitter and Facebook. Another good way to discover sponsors is in the Etsy forums. Etsy is a site that craftsmen sell their handmade goods on. Just post that you're seeking sponsors for a giveaway on your site, what type of site you have and your contact info. Likely the easiest way to pull in sponsors is to begin praising them on your site. Do you love a housecleaning product? A gizmo? Playthings? When you give good reviews, individuals will take notice, particularly businesses. If a business contacts you to sponsor a giveaway, they'll more than likely offer you a gratis product to review. Then they'll provide one or more of that same product for you to have a giveaway with.

All right, now you have your giveaway prize. Begin dropping hints that you'll be featuring a giveaway soon. This peaks interest and keeps people coming back. When you're ready to submit your giveaway, make certain to make it an amusing post. Ask people to leave a comment about the product, what they admire about it, something like that. Then provide extra giveaway entries. For example if they discuss your giveaway on their blog, they receive an extra entry. If they tweet about it on twitter, a different entry. Utilize your resourcefulness, but make certain it all leads back to more views for your site.

Besides promoting on Twitter, Facebook and MySpace, e-mail it to your friends and family and post it on Online-Sweepstakes.com (OLS). OLS is the largest and best site listing for online giveaways and you'll get a lot of traffic.

Choose the winner and send out Your Prize.

Contact your winner and get their mailing address. Ship their prize without delay, and include a courteous card thanking them for entering your giveaway.

Chapter 3

Gain Loyalty By Providing A Stake In The Brand

Synopsis

When the company Vitamin Water chose to set up a fresh flavor, it chucked the labs and focus groups and marking authorities and addressed social media networks.

Intrigue People

Throughout the summertime of 2009, the company pursued and grew its Facebook fan base by asking for ideas from users concerning the name and promotional material for the fresh flavor.

More than a million fans took part in the contest, and famous persons were intermeshed via video clips to prod interest. In the long run, once "Connect," the fresh flavor, arrived on the shelves, there were a 1000000 potential purchasers on the market far more likely to gather up a bottle than they had been prior to interacting with the competition.

Word of mouth advertising has forever been the best (and less expensive) form or advertising and now with social media tools like twitter and Facebook, it's even easier to help individuals spread the word for just about anything, even your products and services.

In a survey a while back by Nielsen online, they demonstrated that thirty-four percent or respondents wholly trusted something when it came from a testimonial from somebody that they knew. Think about it, if your acquaintance come in speaking very positively about a service or product and you have the slimmest bit of interest in it, you will likely ask who makes it or where do I get one. I know I'm like that.

And so if your company or business has a product or service and individuals talk about it off line, then I would be to your benefit to get them to talk about it online likewise. Suppose you own a restaurant and you meet the clients and they have a fantastic meal. Let them know your restaurant is on Facebook or Twitter and share the page with everybody that comes in. Immediately, your buyers may share their experience with you and other buyers online. Now their acquaintances will see it and be thinking, "Perhaps we should go to that restaurant John was talking about last week…"

Chapter 4

Build Credibility By Helping Others

Synopsis

It lifts the spirits to do good things, and if you are able to inspire other people to follow suit, even better.

Help

A well know shoe brand has made it its mission to provide a pair of shoes to a youngster in a developing country for every pair sold. To maximize its donation, the shoe company inspires users who purchase shoes online to share the word of their purchase on Facebook when the sale is done.

It's not surprising that the shoe makers messaging technique works as well as it does. When I purchase an e-book from Amazon or add a film to my Netflix line up, I've little interest in alerting the individuals in my life. If you ask me to alert them about something large-hearted I've done, my concern ramps up.

When I buy a pair of the shoes online, not only do I prefer to brag about my beneficial deed, I likewise want to encourage acquaintances to follow suit. The shoe company wins by making it simple for me, and anybody else, to do simply that.

Choose on what type of contribution you're going to make. This helps narrow your charity options. You are able to donate food, revenue, vehicles or playthings to different organizations. Work out what you want to donate and discover a charity that takes that item.

Choose a cause that's significant to you. A simple way to choose a charity is to donate to a cause that has directly impacted you in some way. For instance, if you have lost a family member to breast cancer, you might wish to donate to the Susan G. Komen Foundation or the American Cancer Society.

Utilize the Charity Navigator site. This resource measures individual charities and may help you give to a charity that's known to utilize its money with wisdom. It likewise separates charities by category for simpler navigation.

Think about a church donation. A lot of churches will take in donations from its parishioners and put the revenue towards a lot of charities.

Determine how what part of donations really goes towards the cause and how much is expended on administration. The Charities Review Council advocates that charities expend no more than thirty percent of their monies on administration, while some other watchdog groups put that estimate as high as fifty percent.

Donate to a region in crisis. If a natural disaster has happened in a country, send a monetary contribution through the Red Cross.

Chapter 5

Have Some Fun

Synopsis

Do something fun and amusing to get people's attention.

Humor

Not to come off like a broken record by giving this following example, but it still rings true: if you do something amusing people will pay attention. There is a concept: that run tests on whether or not a simple item will blend, video it, and shows it to the globe. Will It Blend?

It is a viral marketing campaign comprising of a series of infomercials presenting the Blendtec line of blenders, particularly the Total Blender. In the show, Tom Dickson, the Blendtec founder, tries to blend various items in order to flaunt the power of his blender. Dickson began this marketing campaign after doing a blending effort with a box of matches.

Popular fan petitions for the show include blending either a different blender or a crowbar. It's highly unlikely that either would blend and this likely means that neither would even be tried, because of the nature and purpose of the show— promoting Blendtec products. A demonstration video sporting the anticipated crowbar was cut off by a cell phone, to which Dickson replies by stuffing the entire crew's cells into the blender and blending them instead. The show has tried to blend increasingly unlikely items, like a six foot garden rake and a sealed can of soda pop

The phrase Will it blend has become a net meme on sites like Digg. Dickson has said that the campaign has been a good success for Blendtec. The campaign took off almost at once. They have definitely felt an affect in sales. Will it

Blend has had an astonishing impact to the commercial and retail products.

Blendtec now sells Will It Blend? Products, including a spoof shirt with the slogan "Tom Dickson is my Homeboy".

Dickson has made a lot of national television appearances, including

NBC's The Tonight Show with Jay Leno, on which he blended a rake handle in bare seconds. Dickson likewise made his appearance in the History Channel serial publication Modern Marvels. In the episode World's Strongest III the show ends with a special Will it Blend to prove if he may blend the channel's longest running series in the form of a portable MP3 player.

As far as honors, Will it Blend has been put forward for the 2007

YouTube award for Best Series, winner of .Net Magazine's 2007 Viral Video campaign of the year and winner of the Bronze level Clio Award for Viral Video in 2008.

Also amusing: will it float, and will it bounce.

Be politically correct. This one is non-negotiable, while it might go against the grain of a committed "humorist." Somebody writing stand-up comedy will tend to be "nervy." You don't want that in promotion. Standing back from any demographic slips or unintended estrangement of a group of individuals is a huge part of making a humorous ad blitz, and occasionally takes work as marketers comb through their concepts for any possibly dangerous material.

Avoid gloomy or harsh humor. Again, this sort of humor is the stock trade of some novelists and comedy authors, but it doesn't belong in promotion. It turns individuals off when you want them to be charged up. For a good utilization of humor, visualize the opposite of dark, a sort of peppy, shiny humor that will draw individuals into your work.

Attempt light situation comedy. Many marketers and gadget companies particularly, have been making wide use of this, with all of the funny family spots involving cells, for instance. This sort of genuinely amusing family comedy is a huge draw to buyers, who then associate the product with functional, felicitous families, even if the roles in the ad aren't exactly "happy" with their cell bills.

Consider what sort of humor your particular target audience may find amusing. Are you selling men's or women's products? To what age bracket? These questions are forever at the forefront of promotion and apply to the use of humor likewise.

Don't let humor overpower your message. Make certain the product is forever front and center. Some advertisers push the envelope and abstract this rule a bit; as viewer reactions become more advanced, the product may be set back a bit, and a bit more humor or concept can still draw a buyer base. But don't get carried away.

Wrapping Up

Sometimes when the topic of social media comes up, a collective moan ensues. What if they don't like our product or service? What about damage control? We need to command our message! And so forth.

What's the bottom line for brands concerned about getting social media incorrect? The train is departing the station with or without you. Conversations about your brand are going to occur, irrespective of whether you choose to participate. Don't sit down on the sidelines. Embrace the conversation and engage.

Even if you take nothing else from this book, let me leave you with this: when it bears on social media, recall the golden rule. If you would be put off by a promotional tactic, your audience likely wouldn't like it, and if you find something so exciting you want to share it with all your acquaintances, there's a great chance your audience will, also. Use good sense, and remember that social media networks mirror how we interact in real life.

Glenda Boone

ABOUT THE AUTHOR

Glenda Boone has established herself as an accomplished author, successful certified business consultant and a "guru" to Pastors, Artists and Business Owners across the country.

Serving in the field of Church administration and marketing for more than 20 years, Glenda has worked under the leadership of some of the most notable Church pastors and teachers in the United States including the Dr. Raphael G. Warnock, Senior Pastor of the Historic Ebenezer Baptist Church, the spiritual home of Dr. Martin Luther King Jr. in Atlanta, Georgia; Bishop Walter S. Thomas, Senior Pastor of New Psalmist Baptist Church in Baltimore, Maryland and Dr. Brad Ronnell Braxton, former pastor of the Riverside Church, New York City.

Glenda's broad skill sets and vast knowledge in these fields have enabled her to establish O' Taste & See Marketing & Productions, strategic planning, and marketing firm that specializes in online and corporate relationship development with faith-based organizations. Through her firm, Glenda has developed relationships with more than 1,000 churches as well as an impressive network of ministers, communicators, audio visual service providers, meeting planners and public relation specialists, enabling her to provide her clients with a network of experts committed to providing impeccable services at affordable prices. Realizing the landscape for the preference by which persons attend church has changed, Glenda's focus is now serving as a Lead Coach of "Social Marketing for Churches." In this capacity, Glenda provides online marketing platforms, strategies and social media training helping pastors and staff expand their community outreach and increase donations using Google, Facebook, and Instagram.

A certified meeting planner, Glenda, has planned some of the country's most notable events including the internationally televised 50th Anniversary of Martin Luther King Jr's. March on Washington. Further, she has helped pastors produce logistical plans and Playbooks for some of the most famous and fruitful religious conferences held in the US including Kingdom Conference that was used as a business model to form T.D. Jakes Mega fest Conference. She has had the pleasure of collaborating and or planning events with several acclaimed artists and religious leaders including: Annie Lee, (Fine Artist) Billy Dee Williams, (Actor-Fine Artists) Xernona Clayton, (founder, Trumpet Awards Foundation), Kathy Hughes (TV One/Radio One) , Rev, Al Sharpton, Rev. Jesse Jackson, Bishop Paul Morton, Bishop TD Jakes and Bishop Eddie Long to name a few. Glenda attended Coppin State

University and earned a Bachelor of Science In Business degree with a Concentration in Project Management from the University of Phoenix. She and her husband, Milton, are the proud parents of two daughters, Tarin and Lauren.

www.ingramcontent.com/pod-product-compliance
Lightning Source LLC
Chambersburg PA
CBHW040301220526
45473CB00002B/556